# How to Make Money on Amazon, EBay and Alibaba

*Easy Options to Generate Continuous Streams of Income Online*

# Contents

# Introduction

You want to start your own business online, but confused about where to go or where to begin. Obviously, you need to keep in mind that any business, whether online or not, will require time and resources, therefore, you are not ready yet, until you put these two in place. This does not mean you have to spend too much just to start your own business online, as a matter of fact , it costs nothing to sign up and start making money on Amazon, EBay and Alibaba, as long as you have something to sell, promote or service to render.

Secondly, you don't have to sell anything to make money on Amazon EBay or Alibaba, you can also make money by promoting existing products, through your Affiliate marketing and referral links. You probably have a regular job that takes most of your time, thus time may be something you rarely have, but the good news is that, you don't have to spend several hours online before you can start making money (even 1-2 hour a day should be enough, if you know what you are doing and you have a great medium where you can easily connect with your potential clients).

If you have enough time in your hands, you can decide to sell your own goods on Amazon, EBay and Alibaba. In this situation, you need to know how much time you need to search or get supplies of your products, package them, and ship them. Likewise, you need to keep in mind those shipping fees you will incur alongside other handling charges. However, if you don't have much time to export or ship goods online, you can just find products to promote and sell. In this case, you need to know what products to search for and how to create a huge followership that can be converted into repeated sales, for the products.

You need to do quite a number of researches before you decide which product to sell, because there are lots of junks out there that may never generate a single dollar. You need to also keep in mind that ecommerce websites such as Amazon, EBay and Alibaba and always in favour of customers, therefore any complaint from them means you will lose your rating and possibly the opportunity of making money on a deal.

Subsequent chapters will highlight some of the things you need to do to avoid losses and maintain steady streams of income on the three largest online Ecommerce websites. Likewise, the next chapter gives you incredible figures that should lure you into starting your own business on Amazon, EBay, and Alibaba.

# Chapter 1 - Principle to follow when making money on EBay, Amazon, and Alibaba

Many prospective business men and women on EBay, Amazon, and Alibaba would often ask the question; what can I do to make money steadily on online Ecommerce websites?

The answer is simple;

**Put your prospective customers first!**

You need to have it at the back of your mind that there is no way you can make money online without putting your partners and customers first, and this is the number one principle you must follow.

There are lots of get-rich quick schemes out there, but ask any successful business owner on Amazon, EBay and Alibaba, they will tell you the simple truth, and that is; Putting customers at the center of the business. When you put this principle in practice, you will be able to achieve the following;

- Create, promote and sell products that will solve the problems of your targeted customers. Therefore, you wouldn't focus only on chasing and promoting the hottest-selling products that everyone else is selling.
- You will discover the real benefits of your products to your targeted consumers, and how it can make positive impact on their everyday lives. Furthermore, you will be able to bring these benefits into how your product is presented on the ecommerce websites (Amazon, EBay, and Alibaba), especially through attractive descriptions and images. Also, you will be able to establish strong connections with your customers, by speaking to them directly.
- You will be able to develop a true followership and loyal customers, by selling genuine products, because you have provided them with honest product descriptions and you provide perfect customer service.
- Another principle you must pursue diligently, in order to make money continuously on ecommerce websites is;

## Invest in your existing customers, and more will automatically follow

When you offer little rebates and discount for your existing customers, they will definitely be happy to invite their friends to do business with you and that means more money in your pocket. Just like a popular saying goes "don't bite the hands that feed you". Always stay connected with your existing and loyal customers, and work on the feedbacks you get from them.

## Stick with the rules

You need to take note of many Amazon and EBay accounts that are being shut down on daily basis because they violate policies of the operations of the sites. Do not make any attempt to bend the rules on Amazon, EBay and Alibaba, if you do, you will not only lose your account, but also lose your earnings. Make sure you spend some time to read these rules and understand them even before you start doing business on them. For instance, make sure the Graphics and banners in your product images do not break the rules, similarly, you must NOT pay for positive reviews for your product(this is one of the main reason why accounts get closed on Amazon).

Though, many sellers on these sites have been lucky enough to get away with various cheating techniques on Amazon, but you must not put your means of livelihood and reputation at stake by getting fake reviews to enhance the ranking of your product on Amazon.

## Learn from the experiences of others

In order to achieve success fast on Amazon, EBay, and Alibaba, you must learn from the experiences of others. When you learn from other successful people on ecommerce sites, your momentum and speed to success increases sharply, because you will be able to avoid the mistakes such people have made. You need to consider the following principles and ideas if you are a beginner wanting to make money on Amazon, EBay, and Alibaba:

- Stick with profit margins of between 50 and 100% at the beginning.

- Consider selling products that starts from $20, much higher prices may be preferable.

- Always check the Amazon, EBay and Alibaba listing fees (for instance, the FBA and storage fees).

- Try to re-invest part or all of your profit, until you get to a comfortable ranking.

- Make sure you participate in incentive programs offered on ecommerce sites (for instance, the FBA or Fulfillment by Amazon program where the site do all the picking, packaging and shipping for you), these will save you time, energy and money.

- Make use of the Bar Code scanning app provided by the site, that can give you an indication of whether you can make money selling a product or not.

- Keep tab on the price trend of products you are selling, with the tools provided by the site.

Be efficient and outsource any duty that are quite complex. Stay committed to your online business and you will surely reap the rewards.

# Chapter 2 - Comprehensive Guide on how to start making money on Amazon, EBay, and Alibaba

In order to make continuous and sustainable streams of income on Amazon, EBay and Alibaba, you need to follow a systematic guide that will simplify your work and make the journey smoother for you. These steps are;

- Prepare (know a good product to promote and sell)
- Research(Find the best products)
- Buy ( finding test suppliers)
- Sell (How to sell your products effectively)
- Grow and Expand

## Step #1 : Prepare – what is a good product?

Just like in any other business, making money on ecommerce sites like Amazon, EBay and Alibaba requires adequate preparation, if you want to start on a successful note.

Some people may ask the question; why don't I start selling cheaper products like towels, and sunglasses on Amazon or EBay, considering the fact that they are cheap? The answer to this is simple; selling products that are very cheap will not yield any profit on the long term, especially when you still have to pay charges and fees.

You need to consistently look for single-selling products to sell in order to make profits online, and do not look for a profitable niche to operate in. Your main aim is to create a brand for yourself and branch out. If you want to stick with some easy income, just to sustain your lifestyle, you may not have to worry about branding and branching out, just want to find a single profitable product to sell.

## So, what makes a product, a good one?

Now that you are searching for a single product to sell, you should know what exactly constitute a very good product. There are some qualities that make a product to be good, thus, you must look for those "sweet spots" that make the product appealing and sellable. A good product is the one that;

- Small and light enough to be easily picked up
- Specific ( niche item)
- Selling at between $10 and $200
- Has consistent streams of buyers
- Selling for as much as twice your buying price.

The bigger and heavier a product is, the costlier it is to ship, thus it is better to deal with products you can easily handle and not complicated ones. Try as much as possible to stick with a niche product so that people can identify you easily with it. When you are a "jack of all trade", it becomes extremely difficult to track your customers because they get products from other people too. The best and most consistently sold products on Amazon, EBay and Alibaba, are those within the price range of $10 to $200. These ecommerce markets don't have enough volume to create sizable revenue for products lower than $10, thus it may be riskier to sell such cheap products.

A good product is definitely one that has consistent streams of buyers, therefore, you should not settle for a product just because you had a good buying price, because such a product may have decreasing streams of buyers. Similarly, don't go for seasonal stuffs such as Halloween costumes. Try as much as possible to get products with 100% markups, which means you will get a profit margin of 50% upwards.

A bad product to sell is the one with high demand of quality standards and warranties. A bad product is also highly mechanical. Do not sell products that are imported and sold by giant retailers such as Best Buy or Wal-Mart, rather, go for products with single niche with consistent buyers. Do not promote and sell products that are highly fragile and require special shipping items, and if you plan to sell products such as earphones, don't go for brands that have power-sellers, selling thousands of units consistently, you may not be able to compete with such power-sellers.

Do not sell trade-marked products because you may get yourself sued. For instances, counterfeit wallets, toys and purses with United States trademarks will not get you far but into big trouble. Go for products that will make you competitive on Amazon, EBay, and Alibaba, and not products that are already being sold in thousands by retail giants such as Wal-Mart, and BestBuy.

## Step #2: Finding the best products to promote and sell

Now that you are aware of the characteristic features of good and bad products, it is now time for you to start searching for that special niche that will fetch you continuous streams of income. Fortunately, Amazon, EBay, and Alibaba have provided essential tools that will aid your search. If you don't want to market or sell products already existing, you may decide to sell your own products. For instance you can write Fiction and Non-fiction books and publish them for free on these sites. Amazon can pay between 30-70% commission on each book you sell on its website and such incomes are generated for life.

- Alibaba – Alibaba provides tools for searching for product listings from overseas suppliers. You can use these tools to search for product prices, countries, and many more.

- EBay- this ecommerce site will help you search for what price products are selling for, and at the same time it gives you an idea of the volume and price points at which you can sell a product you are looking for.

- Amazon- You will not only see how much products are selling for, you will also be able to check if you can compete with such. Both EBay and Amazon will give you the percentage at which of product listings, and what prices such products are selling for, and your profit margin. You can use Amazon to expand your search and get more information on each product.

## What you should keep in mind while searching

# Using the Alibaba search filters – when you search for product suppliers on Alibaba, make sure you click "check" beside the Gold suppliers option, this will help you filter out the low quality suppliers, and save you time. This option will also save you from potential scammers.

# Using the EBay search filters- when you search for products on EBay make sure you click "check" beside the Complete Listings button. This will help you

discover at what prices, products are selling and how frequently such products are sold.

# What are you searching for? – Remember, you are searching for good products that can be marked up for at least 100%, within your estimates. Therefore, if you are able to discover a good product with all characteristics highlighted above, and has a minimum of 100% markup, then you can add it to your list.

Here are some tips that can further help in your search:

- Look at random objects around you, and consider those things that has been trending over the years, these may include; Belts, Guitars, Kids toys and instruments, Selfie sticks, and so on.

- Consider looking at those Impulse buys that people often consider buying often. These may include pet toys, novelty toys and shock toys.

- Randomly, you should click in-between Amazon, EBay, and Alibaba. Best random products may include; wedding decors, party lights, cigarette lighters, and decorative pillows. Try as much as possible to think randomly while searching for products on these sites.

- If you are still having trouble coming up with product ideas during your search, you can look up resources such as; Amazon Best Sellers, Shopzilla Top Searches, and EBay top buys.

- Try as much as possible to create a spreadsheet where you can write the products in, remember, it may take 90 minutes or more to complete your searches, and get like 5 top products. Try to stick with 15 -20 minutes on each product search category. Compare each product from each site, especially how cheap or expensive is for the product to be shipped, its refund rates, and whether it will still be bought a month on year later.

- Double-check to ensure that you do not have a bad product on your list. Once you have between 2 and 5 good products, you should find their suppliers and try to buy a sample of each to feel the qualities.

## Step #3 Buy (finding test suppliers)

Now that you have products you want to promote and sell on Amazon, EBay and Alibaba, it is time for you to contact suppliers for such products. Do not contact sales representatives; rather, you must contact the suppliers directly. Try as much as possible to contact between 3 and 10 suppliers.

Just before you contact suppliers, you may want to set up another email that will be dedicated to contacting suppliers on the websites, and make sure you communicate through the email only( if you don't do this, you may get spammed with random products from such suppliers).

# Searching an contacting your suppliers

- Make use of the ideal filters- at this stage, you need to switch your search from products and services to "Suppliers". If you are on Alibaba for instance, make sure you start your search by filtering through the "Gold suppliers", then click on "onsite check" and "assessed supplier"- keep clicking these options until you are left with between 10-20 suppliers (these are usually the best product suppliers you can find on the site).

- Write a generic message when asking for the needed information- open a notepad on your computer and compose a generic message you can send to each supplier. Make sure you introduce the message by telling them about the business you are starting, and then write a request for prices, shipping, and Payment Information.

- Send the generic message to the suppliers- simply go down to your list of suppliers and then click on "contact suppliers", then copy the message from the note pad and unto the message box and click on "send" option. You will be surprised that you will start getting responses within minutes or hours.

- Choose from the suppliers you want to buy from- You may probably want to deal only with suppliers that replied your message quickly but on a second thought , you need to hold on for a while (probably for 24 hours), because the first responses you will get will contain product specs and price sheets. This should give you the highs and lows of each products, and from your comparison, you will be able to streamline the number of suppliers to 2-3.

- Buy samples- for samples, shipping along may cost between $15 and $45, and at this stage you should know the supplier you can deal with comfortably. Check all references given and to avoid being scammed, do all your transactions through PayPal or Escrow only.

- Wait for your 2-3 samples to arrive before making your final choice. It should take between 2-15 days for most samples to arrive, depending on the destination of the supplier. Take note of the fact that items may be different from each other, even though they are the same, but generally you should go for products with the best protection policy, packaging, lower shipping costs and higher product quality. Do not hesitate to negotiate with your supplier if necessary, especially when you have made your final choice.

# Step #4:  Sell (How to sell your products effectively)

This is the stage or step everyone is eager to get to, but you must have followed all other steps before you start selling.  If the quality of product you got from the supplier is what you yourself is willing to pay for, then it must not compromise on good quality standard, and nothing must be missing from it. The product must be able to withstand heavy usage and that is why you must have used it yourself for a while before putting up for sale. Learn to sell few samples first before you buy in bulk from the supplier.

## How to sell your products and make money on EBay, Amazon and Alibaba

#1 List your product on the websites

Make sure you set up a seller's account on each of this website before you list your products. In the case of Amazon, you may need an affiliate account that can be linked to the product you are selling. You can also check the "Completed Listings" of a product that sold the most in the past few weeks or months, and then rewrite the copy of the listing. It is quite simple to sell a product on Amazon, just list the price and quantity and submit. If you are not making many sales in the first week, just compare your product with a competitive product listed by someone else and see what you are missing out.

#2: Ship out your orders

As you get orders, you definitely want to send samples to some special customers too, make sure you add shipping and handling charges to the final price of the product before shipping out.

#3: Evaluate your position and performances.

You should start getting feedbacks on your products as soon as you start selling. If you get some positive feedbacks, then you are on the right track but requests for refunds are definitely not good. As a beginner, a positive-negative feedback of 80-20 is good enough, and then you can work on eliminating the few negative feedbacks. You may have to cope with refunds at this stage until you are able to sell a product with zero refunds, therefore you must use a guaranteed and well-trusted supplier, if you want to keep a high score and reputation in EBay, Amazon and Alibaba.

Though it takes time to get your reputation sustained on the high level, but with regular suppliers of top quality products and more positive reviews from your customers, you will eventually reap the financial reward of your dedication.

# Chapter 3 - Making money on Amazon, EBay and Alibaba, is all about growing and sustaining your marketing channels

Getting a reputable supplier and selling, is just half of the job, without growing and expanding your business. By now, you should be aware of the data and statistics as well as the best marketing channels you can use in promoting your business. You should know how many units of the product you can sell per week and how much you can make on each bulk supplies. Even if you start with selling 2-5 units per week, it shows that you are making progress and it is time to expand and get more customers.

If possible, you should have a website that can promote your brand, even outside of Amazon, EBay and Alibaba. Here are some few ways you can promote and make more money on EBay, Amazon and Alibaba;

- List your brand on diverse existing sales channels – Try as much as possible to list a single product across all sales channels on EBay, Amazon and Alibaba. This will give you a competitive edge in the exposure of the product.

- Develop you own sales channels- It is quite easier to create an ecommerce store and develop your own sales channels, these days. Try as much as possible to list your products on Bing and Google shopping Ads, even if you are not creating your own personal sales channels.

- Advertise on some existing sales channels- One of the best possible ways of maximizing your earnings is to advertise your product listings on existing sales channels on Amazon, EBay and Alibaba. Millions of people see such ads on daily basis, and you can leverage on this.

- Test on new products- as you continue to generate income on existing product, you may have some extra cash to test some new products. Recommend these new products to your buyers and you will eventually increase your customer base.

- Brand yourself- Branding yourself will take a lot of dedication and hard work but the financial rewards are quite excellent. Branding means, customizing your own shipping options, having your own secured payment system and expanding your range of products. Make sure you pick a suitable Brand name that goes perfectly with your line of business.

- Sustain a recurring revenue- The best possible way you can make money on EBay, Amazon and Alibaba is to have a recurring revenue. This means you should consider options such as putting promotional materials in packages or boxes, creating a mailing list and newsletter, and monthly subscription packs, among several others.

- Get better supply bargains from your suppliers- as the volume of sales rises, so also is your bargaining power. Don't hesitate to ask for some small discounts as you order more bulks of products.

- Consider outsourcing part of your business- If your sales increase, you will probably have little or no time to ship all items, Outsourcing will help you share responsibilities and you will get more time to expand your business. You can hire someone to keep your inventory or even take care of customer requests and enquiries just to have more time for your business and yourself.

- Engage in PPC Advertising- The use of PPC and Adwords can be perfect tools to marketing your products and services and generate continuous streams of income online; therefore they must not be neglected. If you can't handle this aspect then you can hire an expert to get it done for you.

- Social Media marketing- Though social media may not be the best marketing channels for EBay, Amazon, and Alibaba, but it can be the best tool for branding and creating awareness.

- Try as much as possible to claim back taxes and get tax-free supplies. In Europe, VAT and some other charges may be levied on goods sent outside of the zone, and this may cost even more to sell a product or service, however, you can avoid these taxes by using European-based shipping companies who will charge you per quantities and without the extra VAT. You can also make use of drop-shippers in countries where extra charges are levied on imported items. Drop-shippers may be found through existing suppliers or online.

## Safety, and other tips and ideas to sustain your investment in Amazon, EBay and Alibaba

Now that you know what it takes to make continuous streams of income from EBay, Amazon and Alibaba, you may want to sustain your business for a lifetime; therefore you need to take note of certain things; Make sure you have an SSL or any other latest encryption for your ecommerce website, most especially if you operate an affiliate website. Fortunately, Amazon, EBay and Alibaba have an effective fraud-control system that protects all financial transactions, but third party websites such as personal blogs are not protected.

## When you should start advertising your business

Though there is no specific time one should start advertising, but experts suggest you should start advertising your business on Amazon, EBay and Alibaba, once there is a significant increase in your sales volume.

# Chapter 4 - Key features you must not ignore about making money on EBay

Making money on ecommerce sites like eBay is all about running a successful business, hence you need to consider all upfront costs and administrative costs, and then monitor your products and services' positioning and qualities, before you think about marketing and promoting your items. Once you have done these, then you can think of the ideal selling price for your items (this can change from time to time, depending on a number of factors). You need to consider how you will process and fulfill your orders and ultimately you need to learn perfect customer service. Here are some of the fundamentals to stick with if you want to make money on EBay;

- Learn about the selling fees on EBay- as explained in previous chapter, there are some several charges you must consider on EBay, as a matter of fact, there are four different types of fees a seller must be aware of on the site;

  - Insertion fee,
  - PayPal fees,
  - Listings enhancement or upgrade fees, and
  - Final value fee.

The Insertion fee is the fee you are charged when you list your item initially on EBay, you will also pay upgrading, especially for enhancing your product listings. A value fee is placed based on the final price of your item, and the fees you pay when withdrawing your payments from PayPal. You don't have to worry about these fees as a seller as you can include all of them on your price list without charging too much.

- Use the right format- There are two ways through which you can sell on EBay, these are;

  - Auction style, and
  - Buy it now.

  In the Auction style of selling, your item will eventually go to one of the bidders, and that person will be the highest bidder. The Auction style of selling is most suitable when the item is highly in demand. The "Buy it now" option where you can set the price immediately and interested buyers can purchase right away. A fixed price will always make your item readily available, and this option is the best when you know the true value of the product.

- Be wise with the marketing of your item- start the marketing of your product with an informative title, and include the right keywords that buyers may use in the EBay search engine. After the title, then you can include some few lines that describing your product accurately. Make sure that the images of your products are close and clear, and you can illustrate the product better by taking pictures from different angles. Make sure the accurate information on size, colour, alongside the conditions and defects (if any), are clearly described.

- Always follow up on the customer after shipping- one of the mistakes sellers make is that they ignore following up on customers. A new customer may be trying out new products thus he may decide to buy other products from several other sellers, and you will miss the opportunity of selling other products to him. Try as much as possible to build a good relationship with a buyer, immediately the auction ends or immediately the buyer purchase the product. Let the buyer know that their purchase is highly appreciated and do encourage them to leave a positive feedback for you.

# How to become a power seller on EBay

Once you have become a consistent successful seller on EBay, you must set your sight on becoming a "Power-seller". Simply put, a power-seller is that special designation you will attain based on your records of selling great quality products and providing excellent customer service. You need to have consistently completed certain quantities of products to attain this status. You need higher sales volume to achieve higher Power-seller tiers, and similarly, you will get top rated seller tag when you get consistent good customer feedbacks.

There are numerous benefits that come with being a power-seller. In order to become a power-seller, you must have sold a minimum of $3000 in more than 100 transactions and over a period of 12 months. You must also meet some minimum requirements including the maintenance of a good account standing and you must have spent a minimum of 90 days on the site. You must also maintain a great feedback with excellent detailed seller ratings, and that means you must have 98% positive feedback from your customers, in the past 12 months, and especially in four major areas; Communication, Shipping, Shipping time, and handling charges. There are five tiers of Power Sellers that are offered based on their sales volume;

- The Bronze- minimum of $3,000 in sales annually or more than 100 transactions.

- Silver- minimum of $36,000 in sales annually, or a minimum of 3,600 transactions.

- Gold- a minimum of $120,000 in sales annually, or a minimum of 12,000 transactions.

- Platinum- a minimum of $300,000 in sales annually, or a minimum of 30,000 transactions.

- Titanium- a minimum of $1,800,000 in sales annually, or a minimum of 180,000 transactions.

One of the benefits of being a Power seller is that you can leverage on your new designation or status in promoting your business and establishing a strong positive confidence in your clients. In addition to the positive reputation you earn, EBay will assist you in customer servicing needs, including the provision of marketing templates, discussion boards, and UPS shipping rate discounts. As a Power seller, you must abide by all policies set by EBAY, and that means you must not manipulate your feedbacks. One of the greatest benefits of being a Power seller is that you will get up to 20% discount on EBay's final value fees and listing upgrade fees. You need to contact the seller information center of EBay for more information on this wonderful opportunity.

## The fact and simple truth you must keep in mind, in order to make money on EBay, Amazon and Alibaba

For most part, just anyone can make money on EBay, but you need to have a solid plan. Just putting up your items for sale on EBay and spending so much on listing fees are not just enough, you need to search for items that will sell. Here are some facts and simple truth you must keep in mind in order to make continuous streams of income on these top 4 e-commerce websites.

*#1. Not everything sells on Amazon, EBay, and Alibaba.* Those items you can ship cheaply will sell faster; otherwise you will have to get a great discount. For instance, items like TV and furniture are bad items you can sell on these sites, considering the weight of shipping- you can get these items around the corner. You may also find it difficult to find profitable margins on items such as clothes, though some people still get great margins on clothes, therefore they are still sellable.

*#2. You need to be thrifty to make money on Amazon, EBay and Alibaba.* You must not spend 30$ just to sell an item worth $10. Though it may be ideal if you do spend more to sell a cheaper item, especially when you are trying to increase attention to the bigger profit margin from time to time. You need to make money on your item, after you subtract shipping costs and other hidden charges. Buyers seem to have become very savvy in using different tricks, therefore it does not make any sense selling an item that costs $2 when the shipping costs 10$.

*#3Never makes the mistake of quitting your job.* It will take a while to learn and understand what to do on Amazon, EBay and Alibaba. In the beginning, you should see these websites as means of generating extra income and not a full time income generating job. You need to consider the fact that , even the items with huge profit spread may not sell all the time , you just have to keep searching for new sellable products.

*#4 Try as much as possible to avoid bad customer service.* If you don't get your items shipped on time, customers may become irate. Similarly, some customers may get angry when you don't send them a follow-up email especially when the shipping of their items is delayed. You need to be fast about customer issues; otherwise you will get a quick and negative feedback. Secondly, any negative feedback on your profile must be clarified and respond too immediately, if not, future potential customers will be skeptical of doing business with you. Negative feedbacks can destroy your reputation, especially when you are just starting out on EBay, Amazon, and Alibaba.

*#5 Spending too much money on listings is another mistake you must avoid at all cost.* Most people will end up spending too much on listings because it is hard for people to pick out their items. Instead of spending too much on listings why not spend more time taking better pictures of your items, and make use of bold and borders add-ons. Listing fees alone can consume all your profits; therefore you must avoid spending too much on them.

*#6 Using wrong marketing strategies for your items.* You need to make use of some marketing tricks, if you truly want to make money from Amazon, EBay and Alibaba. One trick you can use is to bundle several items together as a lot. People appreciate gift packages and creating bundles of items as a lot will definitely help your items stand out. Don't just rely on the standard listing, for your products, though it will save you time but you must add a caption to your listing and that is; why should the buyer buy from you as opposed to the other store?

*#7 stock up on your inventory, as quickly as possible.* Your stores and listings must be up and running always, therefore, you must not wait until your store is depleted before replenishing everything. You must constantly look for good bargains or deals, and there is always something to find.

*#8 Always research your items before spending your money.* High dollar items such as TVs can get you stuck for a very long time, but getting low-dollar items, especially in bulk can be a better option. For this reason, you just need to find items that that will sell at an acceptable profit margin.

*#9 Always start small and don't be tempted into overwhelming yourself by searching for manufacturers.* You can start selling by buying from friends and family and that is much safer, and cheaper than going out to search for expensive wholesalers and suppliers. Until you find a unique source, everyone knows that you are getting your items from suppliers and wholesalers.

*#10 As you gain more experience, you will eventually understand how to gain competitive edge through smart listings on Amazon, EBay and Alibaba.* Make sure you organize your listings and find the right time to start and end such listings. If you become more advanced in selling, you can make use of "Buy Now", and "Reserve price" auctions to make greater gains. You need to take your time and understand how to use auctions through some research. Some of the best sellers on these three websites normally display an item on both auctions and "Buy now" options.

## How to make money on Amazon, EBay and Alibaba without selling

Affiliate programs are the best alternative options for those who don't like selling to make money on Amazon, EBay and Alibaba. As an affiliate, you will make money as an independent publisher, and all you have to do is drive traffic to EBay and you get a commission from any item sold through your affiliate link.

Content publishers can make money through the promotion they give to ecommerce merchants; you just have to monetize your existing web traffic through the referring of online visitors to merchant partners. You need to make use of trackable links in order to make these possible and get paid for your traffic. This is basically how you make money as an affiliate marketer on Amazon.

Similarly, the EBay Partner Network (ePN) is an in-house affiliate program, and it comes with diverse staggering lineup of options for publishers to tap into and make money from. The EBay's affiliate program simply provides resources to users on how they can monetize their websites, blogs, social media profiles, mobile apps and other online profiles through the conversion of visitors to buyers on EBay.

## How to get started

Once you have established a web presence through your Blogs, websites and social media profiles, and have decided that the EBay partner network is the perfect fit for you, and then you must apply to the

EPN. Applying to EBay's EPN is a quick process, as it takes just few minutes to complete. You can search for the EPN on EBay's website. Once your application has been accepted, you will be provided with several tools, including; Banners, text links, and buttons, then you can add all these tools to your social media pages, websites and blogs. You may choose to copy and paste the codes for these banners, text links and buttons to your site directly; hence it is quite easy for beginners to get started with affiliate programs.

If you have advance skills, EBay, Alibaba and Amazon provide access to their API, and such access will help you develop even better customized solutions. You need to choose the appropriate categories of products you can market to the right audiences- these are the people who visit your websites or social media profiles mostly. For instance, if you have a photography blog, why not promote products that produce the best quality pictures, including cameras and photo-films?

## How to make money with the EBay, Amazon, and Alibaba affiliate programs?

Now you want to know how to start making money as an EBay affiliate marketer or simply put, Affiliate. You make money whenever your online visitor clicks your link and gets directed to EBay, therefore your online visitors don't have to buy an item on EBay before you make money. You will even make much more, when your visitor clicks and gets into EBay and then enroll for an auction of click the "Buy Now" button. You will always get a percentage of the revenues generated by EBay, as a commission. The more sales you drive to EBay, the more money you make.

The EBay Partner Network (EPN), commission to affiliates, vary from one product to another, and you also stand the chance of getting a 200% commission bonus each time you drive a reactivated buyer ( those that have not purchased in the last 12 months), or a new buyer to purchase an item on the site. Being an EPN affiliate does not mean you have to do the tracking and reporting, EBay itself handles all these, and there is a portal where you can login and view the stats, including your traffic and earning. In order to maximize your earnings on EBay, you must make use of the provided tools, including; promotional tools, deal sharing on EBay blog and Analytics. You need to set yourself some goals, and then use the analytics available on the EBay website to monitor, test and adjust accordingly.

If you are already a master in creating some compelling contents for your visitors on web, blog or social media groups, then it will become easier for you to make streams of income from the EBay affiliate marketing program. One of the main goals is to entice your visitors to click through your links and get converted into sales, and you can only do this by compelling them to look through their desired items displayed through your relevant website or social media pages. Make sure their overall experience is enhanced.

The Alibaba affiliate program may not be as robust as the EBay and Amazon affiliate program that does not mean you can't make as much money as you can on the latter websites. Alibaba is basically a ecommerce website for selling and buying, therefore, the best ways to make the most income here is to search for the best moving items to sell and you must have an audience ready for such items. You can make more money by linking your blogs and websites to the site and including the links to the items you sell, in such a way that you can create awareness worldwide and your product stands out of the crowd.

The Amazon affiliate program, works just like the EBay program and all you have to do is to embed the links of the products you are promoting in your blog and website contents. In the Amazon affiliate program, you need to set up an affiliate account, which is activated within 24 and 48 hours. You need to keep in mind that affiliate accounts that are not active for 60 days on Amazon are automatically suspended and you will have to register once again. The Amazon affiliate program will always get you busy, and that is why you need to check and update it constantly.

The Amazon affiliate program is one of the largest and most popular affiliate programs in the world, with some individuals making 6 figure incomes consistently. There are no secret to making money on Amazon affiliate program, it requires your dedication and commitment, and choosing the right products through the steps highlighted in earlier chapters of this book. The Amazon affiliate program will give you between 10-50% commissions on a product depending on the type of product you are promoting.

There are thousands of products you can promote as an affiliate on Amazon but don't be tempted into choosing too many, you need to let your visitors associate some particular products to you. The "jacks of all trades" don't make as much as affiliates who stick with very few products.

# How to make money on Amazon

To be honest, Amazon is brilliant at making it incredibly easy for you to make a purchase. This is especially true with their one-click purchasing via their mobile app, and their tempting free shipping offers. Wouldn't it be nice, for a change, if you could figure out how to make them pay you on a regular basis? Here are six ways to make the online retail giant do just that.

Join the Amazon Affiliate Program. If you own a website, blog, or even moderate a discussion group, you have the opportunity to join the Amazon Associates program and earn revenue by directing visitors to Amazon products. Depending on the product, you'll earn anywhere from 4%–10% if the click results in a qualifying sale. It works by Amazon giving you a unique referral url that you post on your site or blog. Then when someone clicks on the embedded url, the referral is tracked, and results in you getting paid if it ends in a purchase.

As with any affiliate program, your mileage will vary depending on how "ready to buy" the people you send to Amazon actually are. The key is to provide value on your site or blog and a reason to make a purchase. For example, if you run a blog dedicated to photography, start by doing a weekly in-depth product review of new digital cameras and accessories and include Amazon referral links in your review. The review should always be an honest assessment and provide content that is better than anything else on the subject. If you oversell, or come off as fake and commercialized, your readers will see right through the facade and click elsewhere.

Sell Items on Amazon "Handmade". The braintrust at Amazon recently launched Amazon Handmade, a service that allows you to sell your handmade wares to the Amazon audience. Currently, for a 12% referral fee, you can sell your handmade jewelry, home products (artwork, baby bedding, bath, bedding, furniture, home décor, kitchen & dining, lighting, patio, lawn & garden, storage & organization), party supplies and stationery on their platform. While

Amazon hopes this new service will eventually become an Etsy killer, it currently offers artisan sellers a large number of potential buyers for a reasonable cost. If production capabilities have you concerned, don't fret, as you can set your own production time (up to 30 days) on every product you make. Also, it's worth noting that product UPCs and professional photos are not required to get started.

Publish an eBook. By registering for free with Kindle Direct Publishing, you can have your ebook published on the Kindle platform within five minutes and appear in Kindle stores worldwide within 48 hours. Gone are the days of cut-throat book publishing where rejection letters are the norm. You can now publish your novel or amazingly helpful "how-to" guide online and earn up to a 70% royalty on your sales. Plus, you get to keep complete control of your publishing rights and have the ability to set your own pricing. Amazon will even help you format your ebook to optimize it for Kindle users. Also, you can opt into the Kindle Owners' Lending Library so Prime members can borrow your ebook, and in turn, help you gain even more exposure.

Become a Third Party Seller. If you shop at Amazon regularly, you've probably noticed that while the majority of items are fulfilled directly by Amazon, some items are actually sold by third party sellers. If you have a niche product for sale, or perhaps are an artist and have artwork you're trying to move, becoming a third party Amazon seller provides an excellent opportunity to reach the masses.

You have the option of signing up for the individual plan, which is great if you plan on selling 40 or less items per month, or the professional plan if you plan on selling more. With the individual plan, you pay a flat $0.99 selling fee per item sold, plus a referral fee in the 8%–15% range of the product's selling price. With the professional plan, you pay a flat $39.99/month with no per item selling fee, but still have to pay the referral fee.

While the 8%–15% referral fee may seem steep compared to other online selling programs, the large customer reach you'll have by listing your items on Amazon can easily make up for the higher fees. If you really want to step up your game, you can have Amazon fulfill all of your orders by having them store, pick, pack, and ship on your behalf. This is a fantastic way to let potential customers utilize Amazon's customer service department as well as have your items become eligible for Prime two-day shipping.

Sell Your Original Content. Another smart way to get paid by Amazon is to sell your original content like DVDs, books, MP3s, CDs, and video downloads directly on their site. This is done via CreateSpace, an Amazon-owned company, and it works by paying royalties whenever your product is sold on the Amazon platform.

For example, if you've produced your own music and designed your own artwork to go with it, CreateSpace will turn it into a "retail-ready" CD with full-color inserts, jewel case, and printed disc face. They'll even assign a free universal product code (UPC) to your CD and sell it directly on Amazon.com, which means it'll be eligible for Prime two-day delivery and incredible consumer exposure. Royalties vary by product category, and range between 40%–60% of the retail price.

Get Paid for Small Tasks via Mechanical Turk. By completing small online tasks via Amazon Mechanical Turk, you have the potential to earn a decent chunk of change. Examples of popular tasks include looking at an image and describing it in 10 words or less for a 10 cent payment, and a semi-detailed product review for a quick $2.50.

While many of the tasks are low-paying, they can add up fairly quickly if you have the patience to wade through the riff-raff to find the better paying tasks. If you work at a job that has regular short delays — a customer service rep jumps to mind — Turk could make for a great way to fill those breaks with tasks that pay.

Score Discounts for Amazon Reviews. Another cool way to essentially let Amazon pay you is to create an account at Snagshout. The site is completely free, and works by giving you access to a large marketplace of extremely discounted Amazon products, in exchange for an honest review of the discounted products you buy. We're talking discounts that range from 50% to 90% off the original retail price. Surprisingly, some of the items are actually free or only cost 99 cents. You simply shop like you normally would, then after the item arrives, you'll be asked to leave an honest review of the product. By doing so, you'll gain access to another plethora of highly discounted items. If used correctly, you'll be getting "paid" via huge discounts on items you'd hopefully be purchasing anyways.

While some of these tips require more up-front work than others, they all have the potential to be lucrative. This is especially true if you have a blog in place and can incorporate affiliate links into your content, or have inventory ready to sell directly to Amazon customers. In any case, the time has come for the folks at Amazon to start paying you on a regular basis.

# Ways To Make Money Using Amazon Associates

Amazon (website url: www.Amazon.com) is the world's largest online retailer and a prominent cloud services provider. The company was originally a book seller but has expanded to sell a wide variety of consumer goods and digital media as well as its own electronic devices, such as the Kindle e-book reader, Kindle Fire tablet and Fire TV, a streaming media adapter.

Amazon Web Services(AWS) is a comprehensive, evolving cloud computing platform. The first AWS offerings were launched in 2006 to provide online services for websites and client-side applications. Amazon's Elastic Compute Cloud (EC2) and Simple Storage Service (S3) are the backbone of the company's large and growing collection of Web services.

Jeff Bezos incorporated the company as Cadabra in 1994 but changed the name to Amazon for the website launch in 1995. Bezos is said to have browsed a dictionary for a word beginning with "A" for the value of alphabetic placement. He selected the name Amazon because it was "exotic and different" and as a reference to his plan for the company's size to reflect that of the Amazon River, one of the largest rivers in the world.

Because Amazon has been widely popular nowadays, a lot of people found ways to earn money using this website. These ways are doable and easy to do. To give you a few ideas, here are 19 ways to help you earn money using Amazon:

1. *Niche Selection Is Crucial.* I'll get to the actual methods I use on my websites in the next tips, but the first thing I want to say is that the niche you choose is the absolute most important decision you can make. I love to target physical product focused niches and keywords

It's easiest to make money using Amazon's affiliate program if the people coming to your website are looking for a specific product that your website discusses. It's more difficult to use a website like my blog here and make money linking to physical products because the people coming here are looking for advice on how to earn money online – not what iPod speakers they should buy.

2. *Link To Products Inside Your Content.* Roughly half of my Amazon income comes from basic text links posted inside the content body area of a blog post or page.

Example: Check out this cool helicopter. I've been covering these RC helicopters for months and I've never seen this one priced for only $25.98 well off it's $129.95 list price (followed by a link).

Simple text links in the content of an article are the most effective way to get web visitors to click. People trust the body of the content on a page more so than any other area of the website and I know this because the tracking data I've collected.

3. *Make Product Images Clickable Affiliate Links:*

The second best thing I've found next to a simple text link is to use images of the product you're talking about and make them clickable like this cool usb missile launcher:

Roughly 15% of my total Amazon income has come from simply making all of the product images on my websites clickable affiliate links. If you're not sure how to do this with the HTML code, I made an image to show you (click here to see it)

## 4. Link To Amazon.com As Many Times Possible

I alluded to this in the previous few tips but I want to make sure you understand that each link inside one of your articles is another opportunity for a visitor to click through and make their way onto Amazon.com.

It's common for me to link to Amazon five to ten times in a single article (more if I'm doing a product review).

## 5. Product Review Articles Convert The Best

Doing a quality product review for a product directly related to your niche is a very easy way to garner higher click thru rates and increased sales, but only if your review is higher quality.

Ideally you contact the manufacturer's marketing team or PR agency and get them to send you a demo unit of the product to review, but this takes a lot of effort and may not be worth it on a smaller traffic site (at first).

You want to convince the reader to investigate their purchase options by the time they finish reading an article, which is why I'll always include links to all of the products mentioned in a review at the end of the article. That way it's an easy transition from learning about the product during your review and then at the end it's time to make a purchase.

6. *Build An Email List.* You've probably heard this a hundred times by people telling you to build an email list from the blogger and internet marketing crowd, but building an email list is way easier on a physical product oriented website.

Why? People don't have their guard up when they are researching a physical product to purchase (when compared to other purchase decisions online i.e. digital goods). So what I like to do is offer some type of freebie like a buyers guide or some type of information that provides more details about the products they're researching.

On the flip side, I'd love for you to join my email list for this blog but I have to be a little more convincing by showing you that I'm a credible resource first.

For my newsletter provider I use Aweber and highly recommend them. Overall I could attribute at least five to ten percent of my total income due to my email lists because I like to focus on promoting products heavily to my lists during the holidays which leads into my next tip.

### 7. Write Sales And Promos During The Holidays

I typically made between $500 and $1,000 a day every day during Black Friday Week, Cyber Monday and Cyber Week. It is lower during other holidays like Mother's Day, Father's Day, Presidents Day, Valentines Day etc. but you can still promote various sales during these holidays as well. I target every holiday because Amazon creates an actual dedicated sales page every time one of these holidays come around. The deals shared on these pages are generally really good too.

So what I'll do is put together an article of all the top products that are on sale in my niche using the tips I've shared earlier like linking as many times as possible, making the product image clickable and then sending out an email to my list etc. to get even more conversions.

For the structure of these articles I like to target a frequently searched keyword such as "Cyber Monday (My Niche) Discounts" etc. because I know people search for "Cyber Monday" and "Black Friday" millions of times each year but they also search a longer form version like "Cyber Monday (My Niche) Discounts" as evidenced by the above traffic graph from one of my Amazon sites

*8. Sell More Products To Make Incrementally More Money*

This one sounds simple enough and it really is. The more you sell with Amazon the more you make AND the higher percentage you earn. During holiday months I will typically hit around the 8% mark which is double the 4% rate you start with for shipping only 1 – 6 items per month. Even if you sold 7 items you get bumped up to 6% and the best part is that this increase in commission percentage is retroactive (meaning once you reach the next level you get to apply the higher percentage referral fee to every product you've sold during the entire month).

9. *Sell Large Quantities Of Inexpensive Products To Boost Your Payout On High Priced Products.* One thing I do is have websites that are set up in lower competition niches where the items typically aren't as expensive and where it's easier to sell these products in larger quantities ($50 or less). Then I have other niche sites that sell more expensive products at much higher prices ($XXX – $X,XXX) that are sold less frequently. So this way I get to use the increased quantity of sales from these lower priced product websites to help me get up into higher payout brackets so instead of making 6% on that high end item I'll get 8% instead.

## 10. Use Multiple Tracking ID's For Each Website

By default Amazon assigns you one tracking ID like blahblahblah-20 but you can create additional tracking ID's here up to a total of 100. If you hit that total you can always ask for more so feel free to be liberal with your creation of tracking ID's for your websites.

You wouldn't install the same Google Analytics code on every single website you own right? Of course not, because you wouldn't be able to tell how much traffic each of your websites were receiving individually. So the same thing can be said for tracking the money you make on your websites (and yet people still tell me they use only one Amazon tracking ID for all of their websites / facepalm). In the past I've gone so far as to create 15 different tracking ID's for use on a single website.

## 11. Use EasyAzon To Save Time And Make More Money With Amazon

One of the ways I've also been able to make good money with Amazon is to automatically populate information from a WordPress plugin that I had developed based on the needs I had for building Amazon centric websites. The result was EasyAzon. The plugin allows you to insert information and affiliate links to Amazon in a much faster way than creating the links yourself by hand from Amazon.com.

Basically what the plugin does is allow you to quickly insert a text based affiliate link, the image of the product as an affiliate link, a product information grid, convert US Amazon links to UK, GR etc. via link localization etc. etc. and have all those things be affiliate links to Amazon.com so it does a great job of improving click through rates.

The plugin is currently only $47 and available at EasyAzon.com

## 12. Insert Buy Now Button Into Your Articles

This is something that EasyAzon could do for you, but if you don't want to spend the money you can simply insert your own buy now button and turn it into an Amazon affiliate link.

## 13. Create A Product Comparison Grid

Creating a product comparison grid for all of the products within your niche and allowing people to sort by various features is a great way to get some additional sales. I've used this tactic on several of my websites and the product comparison page alone can add an additional 5% to 10% income increase for a website.

If you do it manually you'll need to use this WordPress plugin called WP Table Reloaded and what I do is include various columns for information about the product and in the final column I use a buy now button that people can click to see more info about the product.

## 14. Publish A Recurring Deals Post

If you want to find a way to be able to mention products that are on sale more frequently on your website one of the easiest ways I've done that in the past is to just do a weekly deals post. So what I'll do is publish a post every week with the best deals for my niche and then incorporate all of the previous tactics

I've discussed above to link to the products on Amazon.com. Depending on how often you publish articles you could do it more or less frequently (I've seen some websites do these style of articles every day).

## 15. Publish A Monthly Bestseller List

Amazon has a bestseller page found simply at Amazon.com/bestsellers and so one thing I've done on my site is publish a bestsellers list and simply mention the currently trending bestsellers. Generally speaking the cream rises to the top so if you write an article talking about the bestselling products those are likely to be the best products your visitors are looking to buy anyway.

## 16. Use Native Shopping Ads Over Static Banner Ads

Update: I used to recommend carousel style Amazon ads, but they don't exist anymore. When I used them they converted about 3 times better than static style Amazon banner ads. I suggest using Native Shopping Ads instead which is essentially a replacement to the carousel style ads but allows for greater flexibility.

You can display products by recommendation from the content, by search or with other options.

You can create the Amazon Native Shopping Ads inside your Amazon Associates account here and you're able to manually add products or just display bestselling products from a specific category.

*17. Don't Bother Creating An Amazon Astore*

When I created a store page and used the Amazon Astore tool to "build my own store" I found it converted terribly. Less than 1% of my total income came from Amazon Astore pages before I stopped using them. If you're not familiar with Astore's just take my word for it when I say they suck.

I know people like to shop, but sometimes I believe they'd rather just find a resource that tells them what the best deal is instead. Whatever the reason, the tracking data I used to track my Amazon Astore's showed that they routinely underperformed.

## 18. *Use A Website Layout That Improves Conversions*

I've been using Amazon's affiliate program heavily for a little over two years now and the one thing I found through constant testing is that the layout of your website matters when it comes to how well it converts casual visitors into affiliate sales.

Armed with this knowledge you'd think that people would spend more time testing their theme or website layout to determine the optimal way to make money from their website right? Well, I still see some of the worst converting themes around and that's why I actually paid for a theme to be created specifically for these physical product focused websites I had been building.

I spent around $2,000 on the creation and subsequent modifications of Azon Theme. It's basically a theme with a ton of different options that has evolved based on my own testing and the feedback from members of my Niche Profit Course (all customers get Azon Theme and the upgrades for free). You can watch a brief video which covers some of the Azon Theme options here and if you want to buy it there the price is $97 just $10 but you can even get it for free when you sign up for web hosting using my link (See complete details over at Niche Profit Course)

## 19. Just Get People On To Amazon.com

I know 30% of my earnings came from products people bought because I happened to be the one that sent them onto Amazon.com. For example, I sold a watch a while ago for $5,000 and got a $400 commission but I don't even own a website that even remotely discusses watches. This is one of the other reasons why I love using Amazon's affiliate program.

When you send someone to Amazon.com you get a percentage of anything they buy for the next 24 hours (30 days if they added an item to their cart) so if you can just get them onto the website and they happen to buy something completely unrelated you'll get the money for it.

Amazon spends millions of dollars on improving the way they get people to convert. The fact that they provide a custom user experience for every person that goes to Amazon.com based on the buying behavior and viewing patterns tells me they know what it takes to close a sale. Some of the best closing advice I can give is to simply find ways to get your visitors onto the Amazon.com webpage and they'll take care of the rest.

# How to Make Money on Amazon Without Selling?

The way to do this is through the Amazon Associate Program. It adopts the affiliate marketing business model whereby you earn a sales commission whenever you refer a customer to purchase something online from the Amazon marketplace. Here are some steps to help you make money on Amazon without selling:

Sign up for a user account with Amazon by providing some personal information.

You will receive a call from Amazon for verification purposes.

You'll be given a unique associate ID that allows you to access the Associate Central where all your affiliate resources reside.

You can search for the products that you want to promote, get the product links (which has your unique ID attached) and share them on your website or blog.

Amazon is headquartered in Seattle, Washington. The company has individual websites, software development centers, customer service centers and fulfillment centers in many locations around the world. If you are a good writer, you can also make use of Kindle Amazon wherein it would be easy to publish and sell book from different parts of the globe. With the power of Amazon, earning money would be as easy as eating a cake!

# Conclusion

Try as much as possible to combine different money-making options on Amazon, Alibaba and EBay. You don't have to order and get products to sell from suppliers, you can become an affiliate marketer and sell existing products and get commission for such. Always keep in mind that going into partnership with other reputable sellers can also help your business, especially when they promote your product to their customers and you do the same for them.

Even if your business is having a slow start at the beginning, you must not give up because everyone who has a success story to tell on these websites also had the same issues at the beginning. The more you learn from the errors of others, the easier it becomes for you to get your feet on the ground and start making money continuously from the top 3 ecommerce websites in the world.

Considering the stiff competition existing among sellers on Amazon, EBay and Alibaba, you need to ensure that you give your products the maximum exposure they need, in order to have a competitive edge over your competitors. If you use newsletters and mail lists, then you must keep your customers informed about latest deals, discounts and newly added products. Make sure you follow the systematic approach to searching for good products, before you settle for any products and do not be in a rush to add a product to your line of business- you don't want to damage the reputation you have built over a long period of time.

*James Drummond*

# Create a Successful Blog in 5 Days: How to Start Right and Avert Newbie Mistakes

# Social Media: Marketing Strategy: 35 Ways to Make Money (Facebook, Instagram, Twitter, Youtube, Google+, Pinterest, Linkedin, Upwork) for beginners

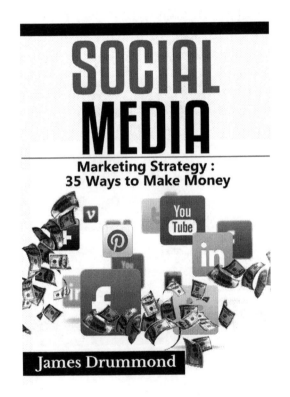

Made in the USA
Middletown, DE
30 November 2016